Duden

Englisch

Erste Texte schreiben

5./6. Klasse

Üben in 15 Minuten

Dudenverlag
Berlin

Inhaltsverzeichnis

1 Tipps und Tricks rund ums Schreiben

Wörter sammeln 4
Auf den Satzbau achten 6
Richtige Zeiten verwenden 8
Ideen und Gedanken ordnen 10
Täglich schreiben 12
Spielerisch mit Sprache umgehen 14
Eigene Texte korrigieren 16

2 Beschreiben

Eine Person beschreiben 18
Einen Gegenstand beschreiben 20
Gegenstände und Personen vergleichen 22
Die Lage von etwas beschreiben 24
Einen Ort beschreiben 26
Ein Hobby beschreiben 28
Einen Weg beschreiben 38
Einen Steckbrief erstellen 40

3 Berichten

Uhrzeit und Datumsangaben 42
Über einen Tagesablauf berichten 44
Eine Unterhaltung schreiben 46
Vom Urlaub erzählen 48

4

Erklären

Ein Rezept schreiben 50
Eine Gebrauchsanweisung schreiben 52

5

Argumentieren

Pro und Kontra 54
Eine Buchbeschreibung erstellen 56

6

Erzählen

Eine Geschichte schreiben 58
Wissenswertes über Märchen 60
Ein eigenes Märchen schreiben 62

Lernkalender 64

1 Tipps und Tricks rund ums Schreiben

Wörter sammeln

Je genauer und ausführlicher ein Text werden soll, desto mehr Detailwissen und englische Vokabeln benötigst du. Lege dir daher vor dem Schreiben eine kleine **Wörtersammlung** an. Notiere dir dafür das Thema deines Textes auf einem Blatt Papier und sammle alle englischen Wörter, die dir dazu einfallen.

Schlage auch in einem Wörterbuch nach und schreibe dir neue Vokabeln auf.

1 **Sammle Wörter zum Thema Fahrrad: Beschrifte die Fahrradteile!**

tyre – pedal – frame – handlebar – spoke – saddle – chain

2 **Überlege: Welche anderen Vokabeln rund ums Fahrrad kennst du?**

____

____

____

3 **Fährst du Fahrrad? Schreibe einen kurzen Text darüber! Die Fragen helfen dir dabei.**

Do you like riding a bike?
How often do you ride your bike?
Where do you go?
What's your bike like?
Do you always wear a helmet?

____

____

____

____

____

____

____

____

So liefen die Übungen:

_ _ _ _ _ _ _ _ _ _ _ _

Auf den Satzbau achten

Schreibst du Texte in einer anderen Sprache, musst du an den entsprechenden Aufbau eines Satzes denken. In einem englischen Satz stehen Verben immer nach der Person oder Sache, um die es geht.
Beispiel: Emma loves books.

Neben der Person und dem Verb gibt es noch die sogenannten **Objekte.** Ihre Stellung im Satz hängt von ihrer jeweiligen Bedeutung ab:

- Angaben zur **Häufigkeit** (*always, sometimes, never* usw.) stehen **zwischen Subjekt und Verb.**
  Beispiel: Tina often helps her father.
- Werden Formen von *to be* verwendet, stehen die weiteren Angaben **hinter dem Verb.**
  Beispiel: I am often late for school.
- **Ortsangaben** stehen immer **vor Zeitangaben.**
  Beispiel: Joshua never goes to school on Saturdays.

1 **Finde jeweils den Fehler in der Wortstellung und korrigiere die Sätze.**

Always we go biking on Saturdays.

____

Anne and Amy visit their brother sometimes in Switzerland.

____

We in summer often a lot of ice cream eat.

____

Our teacher every summer travels to England.

____

2 Emma hat einen Aufsatz über ihre Heimatstadt geschrieben, doch leider sind die Sätze durcheinandergeraten. Hilf Emma, den Aufsatz neu zu schreiben.

Clark – My – is – name – Emma. London – live – in – I.
a – wonderful – My – city – hometown – is. London, – There –
river – the river Thames – is – a – flows – big – through – flows – that.
the Tower of London. – Close – the – is – river – to
stores – The – family – royal – their – crown jewels – there.
Buckingham – is – Palace – an – building – important – too.
there – lives – Elizabeth – Queen.
love – London Eye, – I – the big ferris wheel.
small cabins – You – sit – the wheel –
can – turns – while – in – and – have – you – a fantastic view –
city – of – the.

So liefen die Übungen:

1

Richtige Zeiten verwenden

Bevor du einen Text schreibst, überlege dir, welche Zeit du verwenden musst. Je nach Textform sind unterschiedliche Zeitformen nötig:

→ **Rezepte, Gebrauchsanweisungen** oder **Beschreibungen** erfordern die Gegenwartsform, das Simple Present. Gebildet wird es mit der Grundform (Infinitiv) des Verbs. In der 3. Person Singular wird an den Infinitiv ein *-s* angehängt. Dabei ändern manche Verben ihre Schreibweise.
Beispiele: We all **like** ice cream.
She **says** nice things.
He **hurries** to catch the train.

→ **Erzählungen** und **Berichte** werden meist in der Vergangenheit geschrieben, dem Simple Past. Das Simple Past wird regelmäßig gebildet, indem man die Endung *-ed* an den Stamm des Verbs anhängt. Es gibt aber auch unregelmäßige Formen, die musst du auswendig lernen.
Beispiele: to look – I **looked** at him.
to drink – She **drank** a glass of water.

→ Für **Ereignisse,** die **in der Zukunft** geschehen, verwendet man das Futur. Im Englischen gibt es zwei Möglichkeiten, dieses zu bilden. Das ***going-to-future*** nutzt man für geplante Ereignisse, das ***will-future*** für spontane Entscheidungen, Vermutungen und Versprechen.
Beispiele: Tomorrow I **am going to** walk to the restaurant.
Perhaps I **will walk** to the restaurant later.

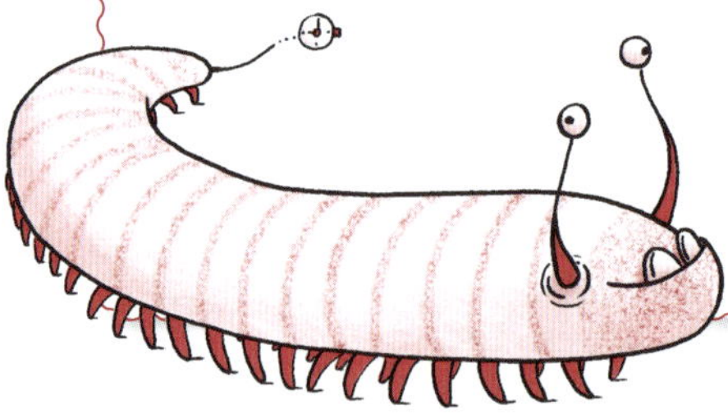

1 **Auf dem Bauernhof gibt es viel zu beobachten. Beschreibe, was du siehst. Setze die Verben in der richtigen Zeitform in die Lücken ein.**

A farm is a busy place. What does everybody do?

The farmer ______________________ his tractor. (to drive)

The cow ______________________ water. (to drink)

The hen ____________________ eggs. (to lay)

The farmer's wife ____________________ the eggs. (to collect)

The dog ____________________ . (to sleep)

2 **Berichte, was du gestern auf dem Bauernhof beobachtet hast. Verwende das Simple Past.**

The farmer drove his tractor. ________________________________

____

____

____

____

____

3 **Fülle die Lücken. Achte auf Signalwörter und setze die richtige Zeitform ein.**

Yesterday, a house ____________________ (is) on fire. The fire fighters ____________________ (work) hard to stop the fire.

The bus driver ________________ (take) the children to school every day.

My mum and I plan a trip to London. We ____________________ (visit) Buckingham Palace and Madame Tussaud's next year.

My dad ____________________ (eat) pizza every Sunday while he ____________________ (watch) football on TV.

Perhaps he ____________________ (walk) to his sister's house later.

So liefen die Übungen:

_ _ _ _ _ _ _ _ _ _ _ _ _

Ideen und Gedanken ordnen

Bevor du einen Text oder eine Geschichte verfasst, ist es hilfreich, eine **Ideensammlung** anzufertigen und die **eigenen Gedanken** zu **ordnen, zum Beispiel mit einer sogenannten Mindmap.**

Notiere das **Thema** oder die Idee **in der Mitte** eines Blattes und ergänze deine Gedanken. Zuerst sieht es etwas unordentlich aus, aber nach und nach entsteht eine Ordnung. Du hast quasi eine **Landkarte deiner Gedanken** erstellt.

Alternativ kannst du deine Ideen auch auf Klebezetteln sammeln. Diese kannst du ganz einfach an eine Wand anheften und beliebig neu anordnen – auch in Form einer Mindmap. Mit unterschiedlichen Farben kannst du zum Beispiel festlegen, welche Gedanken am wichtigsten sind.

1 Erstelle eine eigene Mindmap zum Thema „A day in London“. Was würdest du unternehmen?

A day in London

visit the Tower of London

2 Schreibe nun einige Sätze zu deinem „Tag in London“. Was siehst du dir an? Wohin gehst du? Nutze deine Mindmap aus Aufgabe 1 und achte auf die Zeitform.

On my day in London I am going to visit the Tower of London.

After that ______________________

____

____

____

____

____

____

So liefen die Übungen:

____

Täglich schreiben

Schreiben ist auch Übungssache – also schreibe so viele Texte wie möglich. Vielleicht legst du dir ein kleines Schreibtagebuch an, in das du zum Beispiel jeden Abend **das schönste Erlebnis des Tages** einträgst.
Verwende dazu am besten das *Simple Past.*
Das *Simple Past* wird für eine Handlung verwendet, die in der Vergangenheit liegt und nun beendet ist, und für mehrere Handlungen, die in der Vergangenheit aufeinanderfolgten und nun ebenfalls abgeschlossen sind.

Es gibt Signalwörter, die dir zeigen, wann das *Simple Past* gefordert ist: *yesterday, last week, last month, last year, ago* sowie in Verbindung mit einer Jahreszahl.

Beispiel: Yesterday I had soccer practice and scored a goal! I was so happy!

1 **In Tagebüchern geht es oft um Gefühle. Kennst du die Vokabeln? Finde das Gegenteil.**

excited ____________________ to love ____________________

happy ____________________ to smile ____________________

2 **Versuche dir beim Schreiben Schwerpunkte zu setzen. Verwende zum Beispiel eine Woche lang möglichst viele Vokabeln, die Gefühle ausdrücken. Schreibe hier Vokabeln zum Thema Gefühle auf.**

____

____

____

____

3 Prinzessin Georgina hat auf ihrer Reise Notizen gemacht. Formuliere sie aus.

Monday: fought against a dragon – hated it! Tuesday: watched two robbers digging a hole – saved the treasure – very happy
Wednesday: relaxed – sun Thursday: my horse broke a leg – terrible
Friday: found the castle – saw my dad through the window – excited
Saturday: met new people – the king threw me a party – fantastic

Dear diary,

So liefen die Übungen:

Spielerisch mit Sprache umgehen

Sprachspiele, wie zum Beispiel Gedichte, helfen, dein Sprachgefühl zu verbessern, und sind deshalb auch ein gutes Schreibtraining. Gedichte sind meist kurze Texte. In einigen kommen Reimwörter vor, andere bestehen nur aus einem kurzen Satz, ganz ohne Reimwörter.
Gedichte können Gefühle oder Gedanken zum Ausdruck bringen. Dafür werden unterschiedliche Mittel eingesetzt.

→ Wenn sich in einem kurzen Satz Begriffe wiederholen, wirken diese besonders eindringlich.
Beispiel: At home I have my mum,
I have my dad,
I have my room,
I'm not alone.
At home.

→ Reime geben einem Gedicht einen speziellen Klang oder Rhythmus. Sie können zum Beispiel beruhigend wirken.
Beispiel: I like you, you like me,
That's the way it should be.

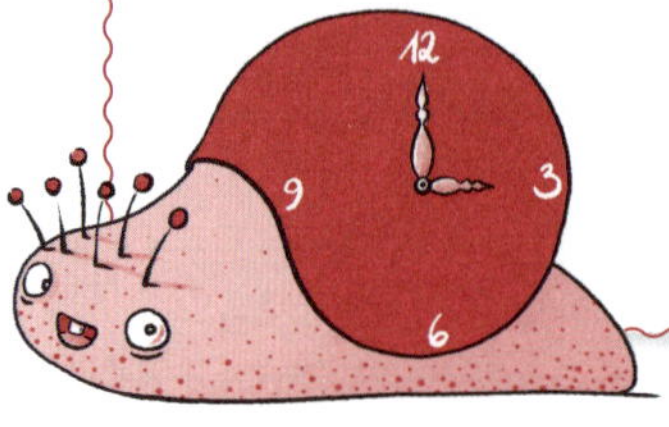

Gedichte schreiben hilft dir, mit Sprache zu spielen und neue Wörter auszuprobieren. Sei kreativ und mach dir nicht zu viele Gedanken. Es gibt keine falschen Gedichte!

1 **Versuche dein eigenes Gedicht ohne Reime zu schreiben.**

2 **Welche Wörter reimen sich? Verbinde die Paare miteinander und ergänze jeweils noch ein Reimwort.**

dear	go	fear
far	cat	
basketball	town	
clown	loose	
head	fly	
shoes	star	
by	bed	
throw	tall	
hat	near	

3 **Schreibe verschiedene Dreizeiler, die sich reimen. Nutze die Wörter aus Aufgabe 2.**

My fat cat
is really mad
because it's wearing a hat.

So liefen die Übungen:

Eigene Texte korrigieren

Du hast einen Text geschrieben? Prima! Hier findest du ein paar einfache Tipps, die dir helfen können, deine eigenen Texte zu korrigieren:

- Denke noch einmal an die **Art von Text,** die du schreiben wolltest, zum Beispiel eine Erzählung, einen Brief oder eine Beschreibung. Jede Textsorte hat einen typischen Aufbau. Lies dir den Text dann noch einmal genau durch und überlege, ob der Aufbau logisch ist.
- Hast du die **richtigen Zeiten** verwendet? Überprüfe, ob es Signalwörter gibt, die bestimmte Zeiten erfordern: Gegenwart, Zukunft oder Vergangenheit.
- Überprüfe dann, ob du alle **Wörter richtig geschrieben** hast. Schau im Zweifel in deinem Schulbuch, in einem Wörterbuch oder im Internet nach.
- Hast du alle **Satzzeichen** richtig gesetzt? Überprüfe Kommas, Ausrufe- und Fragezeichen sowie die Anführungszeichen bei der direkten Rede.

1 **Überprüfe, ob die Sätze zur jeweiligen Überschrift passen. Welche Fehler wurden gemacht? Was kannst du verbessern?**

a) **Missing-Person's Report:** Once upon a time there was a handsome man. He had brown hair and beautiful teeth. Where is he?

____

____

____

b) **Granny's Pizza Recipe:** Put the pizza in the oven. Now, cut the onions and the cheese. Afterwards, put the tomato sauce on the dough.

____

____

____

2 **In diesem Text haben sich 10 Fehler versteckt. Unterstreiche sie und schreibe den Text fehlerfrei auf.**

Henry and the four dogs

Once upon a time, there was a littel boy. His name was Henry. He hat golden hair. One dai, he was walking in the forest. He kame to a little hut. He knocked on the door, but nobody was their. So he went inside.

The boy with the goden hair saw four bowls of soup on the table. He was hungry, so he eated all the soup. He went to sleep in a little bed in the hut. Soon, the dog familie came home.

Mummy Dog and Daddy Dog saw Henry in the dog crib. They woke him up. When Henry saw the dogs he screamed. He runned away and never come back.

So liefen die Übungen:

2 Beschreiben

Eine Person beschreiben

Bei einer Personenbeschreibung beschreibst du die **sichtbaren Merkmale** eines Menschen so anschaulich wie möglich. Ist er oder sie groß oder klein? Wie alt ist die Person ungefähr?
Beispiel: This woman is my mum. She is 35 years old and very tall.

Damit sich jemand die Person noch besser vorstellen kann, musst du sie ganz genau beschreiben. Hat sie lockige oder glatte Haare? Welche **Haar- und Augenfarbe** hat sie? Trägt sie auffällige, sportliche oder elegante **Kleidung?** Hat sie **besondere Merkmale,** wie zum Beispiel ein Tattoo, eine Brille oder Sommersprossen?
Beispiele: My mum has got green eyes and brown curly hair.
She has got a little tattoo behind one ear. It's a star.

Tipp: Wenn du eine Person beschreibst, vergiss nicht, dass in der 3. Person Singular bei regelmäßigen Verben immer ein **-s** angehängt wird.
Beispiel: to wear – She wear**s** blue sunglasses.

1 **Lies den Text und trage die Namen von Lindas Familie in den Stammbaum ein. Zeichne die Familienmitglieder, wenn du magst.**

My family
My name is Linda. I'm eleven years old. I've got brown eyes and I've got red hair. My mum's name is Elizabeth. Her hair is brown, her eyes are green. Robert is my dad. He has long, red hair and he looks like a rock musician. My dad's parents are from Ireland. My grandfather is called Colin and my grandmother's name is Virginia. Virginia wears pink glasses. Colin always wears a baseball cap.
My mum's parents are really old. Grandma Mary has grey hair and Grandpa William is bald. They both always wear crazy pullovers in wild colours. I think Mum's parents are really cool. I love them very much.

______	______	______	______
______		______	
	Linda		

2 Beschreibe deine eigene Familie. Die Wörter helfen dir dabei.

uncle brother sister grandmother dad mum cousin
aunt grandfather tall hair eyes young old

____

____

____

____

____

____

____

____

____

So liefen die Übungen:

______________ ☺ 😐 ☹

Einen Gegenstand beschreiben

Wie bei einer Person beschreibst du auch das Aussehen eines Gegenstandes mit Worten so genau wie möglich. Zu den Eigenschaften eines Gegenstandes, die du beschreiben kannst, gehören die **Größe,** die **Form,** die **Farbe,** das **Gewicht,** das **Material,** die **Funktion** sowie einzelne **Bestandteile.** Adjektive helfen dir beim Beschreiben. Sie geben beispielsweise an, ob ein Gegenstand rund, eckig, groß, schmal oder schwer ist.

Beispiele: a **little** house, a **short** dress, **brown** shoes, **cold** water, a **fast** car, a **fat** donkey, a **thin** book, a **colourful** painting, a **shaped** vase

1 **Welche Eigenschaften fallen dir zu diesen Gegenständen ein?**

window ______________________________

house ______________________________

garden ______________________________

roof ______________________________

sandbox ______________________________

2 **Beschreibe deine Wohnung oder dein Haus ganz genau. Du kannst auch die Worte aus Aufgabe 1 nutzen.**

I live in ______________________________

3 **a)** Lies den Text und überlege, welcher Gegenstand hier von sich erzählt.

Inside of me, there are some books. The books are colourful. My owner only likes some of the books, not all of them. There is a pencil case inside of me, too. Inside that pencil case, there are pencils, a yellow rubber, a red ruler and a silver sharpener. And some coins. Most days there is a lunch box inside of me, too. The lunch box is filled with a cheese sandwich and a chocolate bar. I like my owner. His name is Max. I go to school with him from Monday to Friday.

I am a ______________________

b) Erfinde dein eigenes Rätsel, indem du einen Gegenstand ganz genau beschreibst.

So liefen die Übungen:

2

Gegenstände und Personen vergleichen

Mit Adjektiven kannst du Personen oder Gegenstände beschreiben. Wenn du zwei oder mehrere Sachen miteinander vergleichen möchtest, gibt es verschiedene Möglichkeiten:

→ Verwende die Steigerungsform von Adjektiven (Adjektiv – Komparativ – Superlativ).
Beispiele: long – longer – (the) longest
tall – taller – (the) tallest
Achtung: Manche Steigerungsformen sind unregelmäßig. Du musst sie wie Vokabeln lernen.
Beispiele: bad – worse – (the) worst
good – better – (the) best

→ Wenn du ungleiche Dinge oder Personen miteinander vergleichen möchtest, verwendest du den **Komparativ mit *than*.**
Beispiel: Peter is taller than me.

→ Haben zwei Dinge die gleiche Eigenschaft, verwendest du das **Adjektiv mit *as*.**
Beispiel: My brother is as tall as my dad.

1 **Fülle die Lücken.**

Grandma Elizabeth is very funny. She lives on a farm and doesn't care about her looks. Grandma's rubber boots are green. They are ____________ (small) than Grandpa's boots. Her headscarf is ____________ (big) a beach towel. She usually wears a dress, too. It is ____________ (long) than Grandpa's old sweater. In the evenings she prepares dinner. Her apron is almost ____________ (old) herself. She puts it on and starts to cook. The cat watches her. She loves to eat and is almost ____________ (fat) Grandma's pig in the barn. Life on a farm is a lot of work, but it is ____________ (funny) than life in a small apartment.

2 **Denke dir selbst einen ähnlichen Text zu Grandpa Ben aus. Beschreibe ihn. Verwende dabei auch Vergleichsformen.**

____

____

____

____

____

____

____

____

____

____

____

____

____

____

So liefen die Übungen:

_____________ ☺ 😐 ☹

Die Lage von etwas beschreiben

Um die Lage von etwas genau beschreiben zu können, benötigst du Präpositionen des Ortes.

Beispiele: *in* – in, *on* – auf, *under* – unter, *behind* – hinter, *next to* – neben, *between* – zwischen, *above/over* – über, *near* – in der Nähe von, *opposite from* – gegenüber von, *in front of* – vor

Die Präpositionen geben an, wo etwas geschieht oder wo sich etwas oder jemand befindet. Präpositionen des Ortes stehen meist vor Substantiven oder vor Pronomen.

Beispiele: Our school is **next to** the bakery.
The cat is sitting **in front of** the mouse hole.
Emma is sitting **between** Mary and Sarah. /
Emma is sitting **between them.**
→ Das Pronomen ***them*** ersetzt die Personen Mary und Sarah.

1 **Emma muss aufräumen. Überlege, wo die Dinge ihren richtigen Platz haben, und schreibe sinnvolle Sätze.**

Emma has to tidy her room. Her school bag is under her bed. Her sneakers are on the bookshelf. All the comics are on the floor. Her socks are on her desk. The teddy is lying in a corner of her room. All her pencils are on her bed. Her cushion is in the wardrobe. The picture has fallen from the wall.

Emma's room is tidy now.

2 **Was stimmt hier nicht? Korrigiere die Sätze und schreibe sie auf.**

The horses are hiding under the table. The dolphin is sitting in the sand. The dogs are flying over the trees. The birds have got saddles on their backs. The camel is swimming between two boats.

____

____

____

____

____

3 **Schreibe die folgenden Sätze auf Englisch.**

a) Der Wald ist hinter unserem Haus.

____

b) Der Spielplatz ist gegenüber der Schule.

____

c) Wir wohnen in der Nähe der Bücherei.

____

d) Vor unserem Haus ist ein kleiner Garten.

____

e) Das Fahrrad steht neben dem Apfelbaum.

____

So liefen die Übungen:

____

Einen Ort beschreiben

Um auszudrücken, dass sich jemand oder etwas an einem Ort befindet, verwendet man im Englischen die Ausdrücke *there is* und *there are* – beides heißt auf Deutsch „es gibt“.

Aber aufgepasst: Im Englischen musst du zwischen Einzahl und Mehrzahl unterscheiden!

→ ***There is*** steht für Personen oder Dinge in der Einzahl.
Beispiel: There is one teacher in our classroom.

→ ***There are*** wird für die Mehrzahl verwendet.
Beispiel: There are a lot of books on the shelf.

1 **Beschreibe dein Klassenzimmer. Schreibe acht Sätze, in denen *there is* und *there are* vorkommen.**

2 **Übersetze. Verwende *There is* und *there are* und sage auf Englisch, dass ...**

a) ... es in deiner Schule einen großen Schulhof gibt.

b) ... es eine Straßenbahn von deinem Haus bis zur Schule gibt.

c) ... es an deiner Schule 400 Schüler und Schülerinnen gibt.

d) ... es an deiner Schule mehr Lehrerinnen als Lehrer gibt.

e) ... es an deiner Schule einen Schulkiosk gibt, an dem Süßigkeiten verkauft werden.

So liefen die Übungen:

Ein Hobby beschreiben

Zu den beliebten Freizeitaktivitäten gehört der Sport. Im Englischen werden für die Ausübung einer Sportart häufig die Ausdrücke *to do, to play* und *to be good at / to be bad at* verwendet.

Beispiele: *Do you do any sport?* – Treibst du Sport?
I like to play tennis. – Ich spiele gerne Tennis.
And I am good at basketball, too. – Und ich spiele auch gut Basketball.

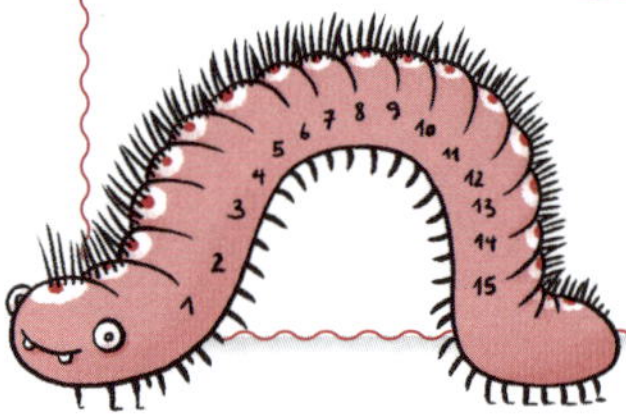

1 **Welches Sportgerät oder Zubehör gehört zu welchem Sport? Verbinde mit Pfeilen, was zusammengehört!**

racket	to swim
football boots	to go skiing
a bike	to go ice-skating
a pair of skies	to play tennis
ice skates	to ride a bike
bathing suit	to play football

2 **Und du? Welche Sportart magst du? Ergänze die Sportarten, die du magst! Schreibe vollständige Sätze und versuche zusätzliche Informationen in deine Sätze zu packen.**

I like:

I like to ski, but only on sunny days.

Tipps und Tricks rund ums Schreiben

Seite 4–5

1

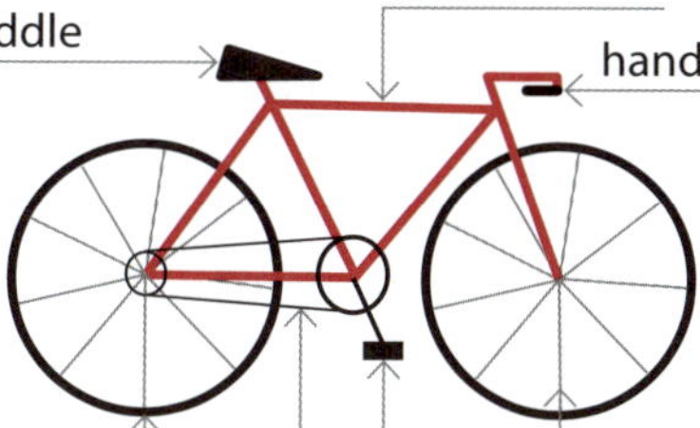

2 Mögliche Wörter sind:
bike (Fahrrad), to bike / to ride a bike / to cycle (Fahrrad fahren), bike ride (Fahrradfahrt bzw. Fahrradausflug), to fix a bike (ein Fahrrad reparieren), flat tyre (ein platter Reifen), bicycle lamp (Fahrradlampe), bicycle pump (Luftpumpe), valve (Ventil), brake (Bremse), mountain bike, gear (Gang), to change gear (schalten), downhill, uphill, bike helmet (Fahrradhelm)

3 Lösungsmöglichkeit:
I like riding a bike because it makes me independent: I decide when and where I go. I do not have to rely on public transport or a time schedule. I ride my bike to go to school every day and to visit my friends. I've got rain clothes, too. I love to be outside. On top, biking keeps me fit: It's a good exercise. My bike is a city bike with 7 gears, it's black and it has got bright lights. I love my bike! Of course, I always wear a helmet.

Seite 6–7

1 We always go biking on Saturdays.
Anne and Amy sometimes visit their brother in Switzerland.
We often eat a lot of ice cream in summer.
Our teacher travels to England every summer.

2 My name is Emma Clark. I live in London. My hometown is a wonderful city. There is a big river that flows through London, the river Thames. Close to the river is the Tower of London. The royal family stores their crown jewels there. Buckingham Palace is an important building, too. Queen Elizabeth lives there. I love London Eye, the big ferris wheel. You can sit in small cabins while the wheel turns, and you have a fantastic view of the city.

Seite 8–9

1 The farmer **drives** his tractor.
The cow **drinks** water.
The hen **lays** eggs.
The farmer's wife **collects** the eggs.
The dog **sleeps.**

2 The cow **drank** water.
The hen **laid** eggs.
The farmer's wife **collected** the eggs.
The dog **slept.**

3 Yesterday, a house **was** on fire. The fire fighters **worked** hard to stop the fire.
The bus driver **takes** the children to school every day.
My mum and I plan a trip to London. We **are going to visit** Buckingham Palace and Madame Tussaud's next year.

L

My dad **eats** pizza every Sunday while he **watches** football on TV.
Perhaps he **will walk** to his sister's house later.

Seite 10–11

2 Lösungsmöglichkeit:
On my day in London I am going to visit the Tower of London. After that I am going to walk across Tower Bridge and back. Then I am going to take the underground, the London tube, to travel to Knightsbridge. There, I am going to go shopping at Harrod's, the famous department store. I am going to take a short rest in Regent's Park afterwards and enjoy the walk to Buckingham Palace. That's an impressive building.
Finally, I am going to take one of London's red busses. I will be tired of walking, and the view from the upper deck is fantastic!

Seite 12–13

1 excited – calm, happy – unhappy, to love – to hate, to smile – to weep / to cry

2 Mögliche Wörter sind: happy, sad, angry, excited, good, glad, great, surprised, proud, safe, fantastic, scared, terrible, nervous, embarrassed, bored, lonely, worried

3 Dear diary,
On Monday, I fought against a dragon – I hated it.
Tuesday was a good day: I watched two robbers digging a hole. When they left, I saved the treasure. I was very happy.
Wednesday was a sunny day. I relaxed.
On Thursday, my horse broke a leg. It was a terrible day.
On Friday, I finally found the castle and I could see my dad through the window. I was really excited.
On Saturday, I met new people, because the king threw me a party. It was fantastic. What a week!

Seite 14–15

1 Lösungsmöglichkeit:
My friends.
My friends make me happy.
My friends are fun.
We talk. We laugh. We play.
My friends and I.

2 dear – near – fear
far – star – car
basketball – tall – fall – call
clown – town – crown – brown
head – bed – bread
shoes – loose – use – news
by – fly – why – cry
throw – go – snow – window
hat – cat – fat – mad – sad – bad

3 Lösungsmöglichkeiten:
My shoes
are loose.
Lousy loose shoes.

The funny clown
comes to town
wearing a crown.

The boy
is tall.
He plays basketball.

A clown
is in our town.
He wears brown.

Seite 16–17

1 a) **Missing-Person's Report**
Die Beschreibung der vermissten Person verwendet Formulierungen, die in einem Märchen vorkommen. Die Beschreibung sollte neutraler sein und die Merkmale des Mannes genauer schildern. Es müssen

Haarfarbe, Augenfarbe, Größe, Frisur und die Farbe seiner Kleidung genannt werden.

b) Granny's Pizza Recipe
Die Reihenfolge der einzelnen Schritte stimmt nicht. Außerdem fehlen die konkreten Angaben zu den Zutaten. Wie entsteht der Teig, wie viele Tomaten benötigt man und wie heiß muss man den Ofen einstellen?

2 Henry and the four dogs
Once upon a time, there was a **little** boy. His name was Henry. He **had** golden hair.
One **day,** he was walking in the forest. He **came** to a little hut. He knocked at the door, but nobody was **there.** So he went inside.
The boy with the **golden** hair saw four bowls of soup on the table. He was hungry, so he **ate** all the soup. He went to sleep in a little bed in the hut. Soon, the dog **family** came home. Mummy Dog and Daddy Dog saw Henry in the dog crib. They woke him up.
When Henry saw the dogs he screamed. He **ran** away and never **came** back.

Beschreiben

Seite 18–19

1 Mary William Virginia Colin
Elizabeth Robert
Linda

2 Beschreibe das Aussehen deiner Familie genau. Welche Haarfarbe haben sie? Wie groß sind sie? Welche Kleidung tragen sie und welche Augenfarbe haben sie? Und natürlich darfst du ihre Namen nicht vergessen.

Seite 20–21

1 **window:** made of glass, translucent, big, small, can be opened, wooden frame
house: big, small, tiny, a lot of rooms, cosy, beautiful, bathroom, bedroom, kitchen, living room, roof, window, door, modern, old
garden: grass, pond, tree, apple tree, playhouse, flowers, bushes, big, small, water hose, watering can, flower pot, garden tools, green, colourful, insects, water, spade, bucket
roof: house, on top of a house, tile, wood, metal, patio, modern, flat, solar panel, pergola
sandbox: children, sand, to build, sand castle, shovel, bucket, sunshine, water

3 a) I am a school bag / a satchel.

Seite 22–23

1 Grandma Elizabeth is very funny. She lives on a farm and doesn't care about her looks.
Grandma's rubber boots are green. They are **smaller** than Grandpa's boots. Her headscarf is **as big as** a beach towel. She usually wears a dress, too. It is **longer** than Grandpa's old sweater.
In the evenings she prepares dinner. Her apron is almost **as old as** herself. She puts it on and starts to cook. The cat watches her.
She loves to eat and is almost **as fat as** Grandma's pig in the barn.
Life on a farm is a lot of work, but it is **funnier** than life in a small apartment.

2 Lösungsmöglichkeit:
Grandpa Ben is not as funny as Grandma. He is a bit grumpy. Every morning, he puts on his dirty working boots. They are older than Grandma's boots. Grandpa likes to look after the farm animals. He likes the pigs better than the cows. He always wears the same, thick green overall and a sweater. His cap is as brown as the earth. I think it's ugly. Grandpa's hair is not very tidy but he has wonderful, dark brown eyes. They are as dark as chocolate. I love grumpy Grandpa.

L

Seite 24–25

1 Lösungsmöglichkeit:
Emma's room is tidy now. Her school bag is under her desk. Her sneakers are on the floor next to the door. All the comics are on the bookshelf. Her socks are in the wardrobe. The teddy is sitting in a corner of her bed. All her pencils are in the pencil case on her desk. Her cushion is on her bed. The picture is hanging on the wall.

2 The dogs are hiding under the table. The camel is sitting in the sand. The birds are flying over the trees. The horses have got saddles on their backs. The dolphin is swimming between two boats.

3 a) The forest is behind our house.
b) The playground is opposite from the school.
c) We live close to the library.
d) In front of our house is a small garden.
e) The bike stands next to the apple tree.

Seite 26–27

1 Lösungsmöglichkeit:
My classroom is quite small. In my classroom there are 10 tables and 12 chairs. Opposite the door there are two big windows. We have a computer in the classroom. On the wall there is a poster of Harry Potter. Next to the smartboard there is a bin. There are two bookshelves in our classroom, too. We are a small class so the 12 chairs are enough.
I share a table with my best friend Lisa.

2 a) In my school there is a big school yard.
b) There is a tram from my house to our school.
c) There are 400 pupils at my school.
d) At my school there are more female teachers than male ones.
e) At my school there is a kiosk that sells sweets.

Seite 28–37

1 racket – to play tennis, football boots – to play football, a bike – to ride a bike, a pair of skies – to go skiing, ice skates – to go ice skating, bathing suit – to swim

2 Lösungsmöglichkeiten:
I like:
I like to ride a bike, especially a mountain bike.
I love to go skiing, even if it is really cold.
I love to swim, but not indoors. I prefer to swim in lakes or in the ocean.
I like to play tennis and I like to win a match.

I don't like:
I don't like to swim, because I don't like to get wet.
I don't like to ski, but I love my snowboard.
I don't like football, I prefer basketball.
I don't like ice skating because I often fall.

3 Zoe doesn't play ice hockey, but she does gymnastics.
Sean likes climbing and surfing.
Emily doesn't play cricket, but she plays football.
Oscar doesn't like skiing, but he likes ice-skating.

Seite 38–39

1 bridge – Brücke, right – rechts, church – Kirche, street – Straße, to go past – vorbeigehen, river – Fluss, left – links, straight / straight on – geradeaus, to turn – abbiegen, police station – Polizei

2 Mina: "Excuse me, could you please tell me the way to the church?"
Mrs Smith: "Oh, that's easy. We are on River Street. Walk down to the end, until you see the river. **Turn right** until you reach the bridge. Go **straight** over the bridge. **Turn left** and walk to Main Street. You can see the

elementary school **on the left.** At the next corner, you **turn right.** Walk until you reach the shopping centre. Now **turn left.** You can see the church **across** the street."
Mina: "Oh, that's a long way. I hope I will remember it."
Mrs Smith: "Well, if you get lost, just ask again."
Mina: "Okay, you're right. Thank you."

Seite 40–41

1 Animal Fact File
Name: elephant
Type: mammal
Home: Africa or Asia
Habitat: near water, in savannahs, deserts, marshes and forests
Food: only plants
Life span: up to 70 years
Prominent feature: ivory tusks

2 Lösungsmöglichkeit:
Elephants are big, grey animals. They are mammals, which mean that their babies need to be fed by their mothers after being born. They live in Africa or in Asia. The Asian elephants are smaller than their African "brothers and sisters". Their ivory tusks are big and impressive. They make elephants very special.
Elephants live in herds. The herd is like a family. They live close to water, in savannahs, deserts, marshes and forests. Elephants can become quite old – they can live up to 70 years.

3 What type of animal is it?
Where does it live?
What does it eat?
What does it look like?
How long does it live?
Why is it special?

Berichten

Seite 42–43

1 Lösungsmöglichkeit:
Dear Mum and Dad,
Summer camp is great. I have so much fun here with my friends. On Mondays, we have a yoga lesson at 5 p.m. Tuesdays are beach days. We can go swimming and play beach volleyball. I even like the kitchen work on Wednesdays. At 11 a.m. we prepare all our meals ourselves. Thursday is our creative day. We can do pottery or paintings or join a stage production. On Fridays, we take the bus to the town nearby. There we do some shopping and eat ice cream. Saturdays are reserved for volunteer work in the community garden. It is so nice that it's summer, because the garden looks beautiful. On Sundays we relax. We listen to music, talk to the other kids at camp and just hang out.

2 Lösungsmöglichkeit: Mimi starts school at 8.05 a.m. Her first lesson is maths. Afterwards she has got an English class. Her first break is at 9.35 a.m. and it takes 15 minutes. After break, Mimi studies history and then geography. At 11.25 a.m., it's time for a second break which only lasts ten minutes. Mimi goes back to class to study French at 11.35 a.m. Her last lesson is PE. It starts at 12.20 a.m. and ends at 1.10 p.m.

Seite 44–45

1 I have breakfast.
I brush my teeth.
I take the bus to school.
I do my homework.
I have lunch.
I get up at seven o'clock.
I go to the playground.
I have dinner.

2 Lösungsmöglichkeit:
I get up at seven o'clock. Then I brush my teeth. Afterwards, I have breakfast. Then, I take the bus to school. At noon, I have lunch. Afterwards, I do my homework. At 3:30 p.m. I go to the playground.
In the evening, I have dinner.

Seite 46–47

1 *Hello!* – Hallo! / Guten Tag!
Have a nice day! – Einen schönen Tag noch!
Hi there! – Hallo!
Welcome! – Herzlich Willkommen!
Good bye! / Bye-bye! – Tschüss!

2 Hannah: "**Good morning,** Mrs Rose."
Mrs Rose: "**Good morning,** my dear."
Hannah: "Could I have two kilos of potatoes, please? And that's all for today."
Mrs Rose: "Of course. Here are the potatoes. That is 2.10 €, please."
Hannah: "There you are. Thank you very much. **Bye-bye.**"
Mrs Rose: **"Have a nice day. Bye-bye."**

3 Lösungsmöglichkeiten:
a) Mary: "Look! There's a book on the floor. Whose book is it?"
Sarah: "Oh, that's mine. It's an interesting crime story. You should read it, too."
Mary: "Thanks a lot."
b) Mum: "Why do you watch this show?"
Tim: "There are interesting guests. Have a look. That's my favourite actor."
Mum: "Oh yeah. That actor is interesting. Can we watch it together?"

Seite 48–49

1 **Dear** Jason,
How are you? I'm **fine.** Italy is great. The weather is **fantastic.** In the morning, we usually **have** a big **breakfast.** After breakfast, we walk to the beach and **go** for a swim in the ocean. In the **afternoon** we sometimes go to little **towns** by bus. We sit down in one of the cafés and have some **ice cream.** In the evening we often **play** cards. Sometimes we play table tennis.
Love, Sarah

Erklären

Seite 50–51

1
1 Prepare the pizza dough.
4 Spread the dough on the baking tray.
3 Cover a baking tray with baking parchment.
8 Enjoy!
5 Cover your pizza with tomato sauce, mushrooms, peperoni, garlic, olives or whatever you like.
6 Sprinkle mozzarella or grated cheese on top of the pizza.
2 Preheat the oven.
7 Bake the pizza in the oven. Be careful not to burn it.

2 Prepare the pizza dough. Preheat the oven. Cover a baking tray with baking parchment. Spread the dough on the baking tray. Cover your pizza with tomato sauce, mushrooms, peperoni, garlic, olives or whatever you like. Sprinkle mozzarella or grated cheese on top of the pizza. Bake the pizza in the oven. Be careful not to burn it. Enjoy!

3 Lösungsmöglichkeit:
My friend likes crisps and salami.
My mum loves chocolate and strawberries.

Alex only eats green vegetables and parsley.
I like a lot of everything: mushrooms, cheese, ham, vegetables …

Seite 52–53

1
1 Healthy teeth make a nice smile.
2 It is therefore very important to brush your teeth.
3 Brush your teeth two times a day.
4 You need a toothbrush and some toothpaste.
5 Put some toothpaste on the brush.
6 Brush your bottom teeth first.
7 Brush in small circles, first the outside of your teeth, then the inside.
8 Brush the biting surface, too.
9 Then brush your top teeth in the same order: outside, inside, biting surface.
10 Now smile and remember to go to the dentist twice a year.

2 Lösungsmöglichkeit:
Take the cards and shuffle them. Put the cards on the table. The back sides must be up. Now start looking for two matching cards. Reveal two cards. If they show the same picture, you can take the pair and start looking for another one. If the pictures don't match, you turn them around again. Now it's the other player's turn. The person with the most pairs at the end wins.

Argumentieren

Seite 54–55

1 Lösungsmöglichkeit:
It is good to have a brother or a sister because then my parents focus on my sibling too and I can do what I want.
It is good to have a sister or a brother because we learn how to share our stuff.
It is good to have a sister or a brother because I always have a friend to play with.

I like to be a single child because I have a lot of friends who I can spend time with whenever I like.
I like to be a single child because siblings often fight and can be really mean.

2 Lösungsmöglichkeit:
I love to go to the circus! It is a wonderful form of entertainment, all the artists are so fantastic. And the animals are funny. Circus shows are very exciting, especially the acrobatics. I also think that all artists who work with animals really love them – the animals are their partners, and human being and animal have to trust and to rely on each other. However, if wild animals are kept in a cage, I believe it is hard for them. I understand that some people would like to free those animals. However, those animals are not used to live in the wild – so freeing them could kill them.
Maybe, in the future, a circus shouldn't show animals.

Seite 56–57

1 A love story: romantic, tragic, no happy ending
A fairy tale: exciting, magic
A fantasy novel: exciting, thrilling
A detective novel: thrilling, exciting, fascinating
Historical novels: realistic, historic, boring, old fashioned

2 Beispiellösung:
Title and Author: "Matilda" by Roald Dahl
What's the book about? The book is about a very clever girl named Matilda who loves to read and to learn. Unfortunately, she is born into a family that doesn't give her the attention she deserves and needs. Luckily, her teacher Miss Honey takes care of Matilda

who one day discovers that she can move things and objects by extremely focusing her mind. This power pushes her self-esteem. When Miss Honey offers to adopt Matilda as her daughter, the girl is finally happy.
My favourite character is Miss Honey because she made her way through many odds and now not only leads an independent life, but also helps Matilda to ensure a better future for her.
I like the book because the story emphasizes the importance of being nice, especially to children.

Erzählen

Seite 58–59

1

Character	Solution
Mia	after the break, the purse is in Mia's school bag
Problem	**Setting**
misses her purse, can't buy snack	at school

2 Lösungsmöglichkeit:
She's wondering – I could buy myself a nice breakfast, but it won't taste good. I will try to put the purse back in Mia's school bag. Nobody will ask any questions.
So Tara secretly stays inside the classroom. She hides behind the coat rack and puts the purse back. When her classmates come back, she simply sits down at her desk. Nobody noticed that she didn't go outside. Mia finds her purse and is very happy.

Seite 60–61

1 fairy tale – Märchen, dragon – Drache, spell – Zauberspruch, wand – Zauberstab, magic (adj) – zauberhaft, magisch, magic (noun) – Zauberei, Magie, witch – Hexe, sorcerer – Zauberer

2 a) Cinderella loses **a shoe.**
b) In the fairy tale "The wolf and the seven little goats", the wolf eats **six goats.**
c) Sleeping Beauty wakes up after **one hundred years.**
d) The Queen gives Snow White **an apple** to eat.
e) Bremen's Town Musicians are **a donkey, a dog, a cock, a cat.**
f) The Frog King marries **a princess.**

3 **Fairy Tale Fact Sheet**
Lösungsmöglichkeit:
Beginning sentence: A fairy tale starts with the words "Once upon a time …".
Magic characters: The magic characters in a fairy tale can be a flying witch or a sorcerer with his magic stones.
Magic creatures: A talking dragon or a mean fairy bring a lot of trouble to a fairy tale.
Magic places: A lot of fairy tales take place in caves, castles or a forest.
Magic things: A witch or a sorcerer can use a magic wand to turn a prince into a frog.

Seite 62–63

Hier gibt es viele verschiedene Lösungsmöglichkeiten. Um deine eigenen Texte zu korrigieren, schau auch noch einmal bei den Tipps auf Seite 16–17 nach.

I don't like:

I don't like to play football, but I like to watch TV.

3 **Welche Sportarten betreiben die Kinder? Notiere deine Antworten.**

Lucas	~~badminton~~	swimming
Zoe	gymnastics	~~ice hockey~~
Sean	climbing	surfing
Emily	football	~~cricket~~
Oscar	~~skiing~~	ice-skating

Lucas doesn't play badminton, but he loves swimming.

So liefen die Übungen:

2

Einen Weg beschreiben

Wenn du in einer fremden Stadt unterwegs bist – oder dir in deiner Stadt Touristen begegnen –, ist es hilfreich, auf Englisch einen Weg beschreiben zu können. Die notwendigen Vokabeln dafür sind:

- **auffallende Orte**
  Beispiele: a church, a bridge, a square
- **Richtungsangaben**
  Beispiele: left, right, straight
- **Präpositionen der Richtung**
  Beispiele: *across* – über, *behind* – hinter, *against* – gegen, *along* – entlang, *down* – hinunter, *from* – aus, von, *into* – in/hinein, *onto* – auf, *out of* – aus/heraus, *over* – über, *past* – vorbei, *round* – um/herum, *through* – durch, *to* – nach/zu, *towards* – auf (etwas) zu, *up* – hinauf

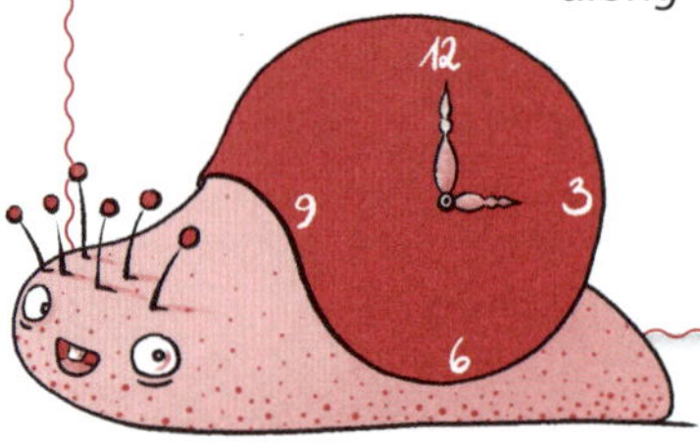

1 **Hier ist etwas durcheinandergeraten. Verbinde die richtige deutsche Übersetzung zum jeweiligen Wort in der linken Spalte.**

bridge	geradeaus
right	abbiegen
church	links
street	rechts
to go past	Fluss
river	vorbeigehen
left	Kirche
straight / straight on	Polizei
to turn	Straße
police station	Brücke

2 **Mina fragt nach dem Weg zur Kirche. Ergänze die Wörter.**

turn left – turn right – straight – turn left – on the left – turn right – across

Mina: "Excuse me, could you please tell me the way to the church?"

Mrs Smith: "Oh, that's easy. We are on River Street. Walk down to the end until you see the river. ________________ until you reach the bridge. Go ________________ over the bridge. ________________ and walk to Main Street. You can see the elementary school ________________. At the next corner, you ________________. Walk until you reach the shopping centre. Now ________________. You can see the church ________________ the street."

Mina: "Oh, that's a long way. I hope I will remember it."

Mrs Smith: "Well, if you get lost, just ask again."

Mina: "Okay, you're right. Thank you."

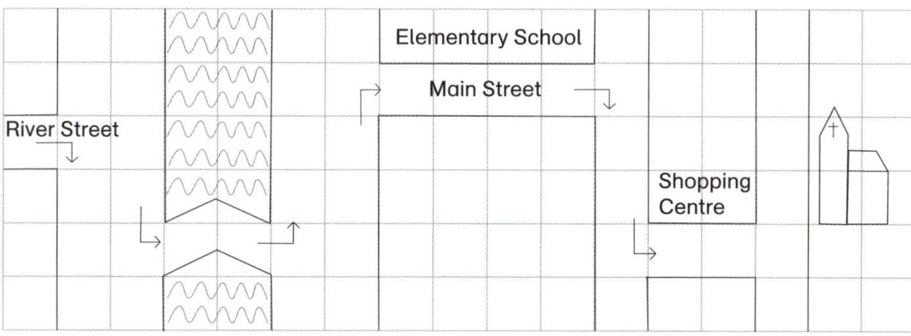

So liefen die Übungen:

____

2

Einen Steckbrief erstellen

Ein **Steckbrief** gibt wichtige Informationen in kurzen Stichworten wieder. Da Steckbriefe die Fakten übersichtlich darstellen sollen, ist es wichtig, kurz und knapp zu formulieren.

Folgende Tipps helfen dir dabei:

- Schreibe keine ganzen Sätze.
- Überlege, welche Informationen am wichtigsten sind.
- Überlege, für welchen Anlass der Steckbrief gedacht ist. Sind alle Informationen nötig?

1 **Fülle den Steckbrief aus. Trage die Informationen an der richtigen Stelle ein.**

elephant - Africa or India - only plants - mammal - near water - in savannahs, deserts, marshes and forests - up to 70 years - ivory tusks

Animal Fact File

Name: ______________________________

Type: ______________________________

Home: ______________________________

Habitat: ______________________________

____

Food: ______________________________

Life span: ______________________________

Prominent feature: ______________________________

____

2 **Formuliere den Steckbrief aus. Schreibe ganze Sätze.**

____

____

____

____

____

____

3 **Welche Fragen helfen bei der Erstellung eines Steckbriefs? Setze sie zusammen.**

it / is / animal / type / What / of / ?

____

Where / live / it / does / ?

____

eat / What / it / does / ?

____

like / look / ? / does / What / it

____

live / long / it / ? / does / How

____

special / Why / ? / is / it

____

So liefen die Übungen:

____

3 Berichten

Uhrzeit und Datumsangaben

Im Englischen wird der Tag in zwei Einheiten von je zwölf Stunden unterteilt. Die vollen Stunden von Mitternacht bis Mittag werden mit ***a. m.*** (*ante meridiem,* lat. für vormittags) bezeichnet. Die vollen Stunden von Mittag bis Mitternacht erhalten den Zusatz ***p. m.*** (*post meridiem,* lat. für nachmittags). Mitternacht (0.00 Uhr) und Mittag (12.00 Uhr) lassen sich so nicht ausdrücken. Man bezeichnet diese Zeiten als *noon* – Mittag und *midnight* – Mitternacht.

Beispiele: 7.30 a. m. → 7.30 Uhr
7.30 p. m. → 19.30 Uhr

Datumsangaben kann man auf unterschiedliche Arten schreiben: erst den Monat und dann den Tag, oder umgekehrt. Das Jahr steht immer am Schluss.

Beispiele: February 1st, 2021
21st February, 2021

Auch die englischen **Wochentage** sind wichtig.

Beispiele: Monday, Tuesday, Wednesday, Thursday, Friday, Saturday, Sunday

1 **Ginny ist mit ihrer Schulklasse vier Wochen im Summer Camp. Sie hat alle regelmäßigen Termine in ihrem Kalender notiert. Heute schreibt sie ihren Eltern eine E-Mail und berichtet über ihre Woche.**

Tipp: Regelmäßige Aktivitäten schreibt man im Simple Present.

Monday	5 p. m. yoga lesson
Tuesday	beach day: swimming, beach volleyball
Wednesday	kitchen work: 11 a. m. prepare all meals
Thursday	arts and crafts
Friday	fun in town: shopping, ice cream
Saturday	community garden work
Sunday	time to relax

Dear Mum and Dad,
Summer camp is great. I have so much fun here with my friends.

On Mondays, we have a yoga lesson at 5 p.m.

1 2 3 4 5 6

2 **Ein ganz normaler Schultag. Schau dir Mimis Stundenplan an und schreibe ganze Sätze. Verwende dabei auch die Zeitangaben.**

8.05–8.50	maths	10.40–11.25	geography
8.50–9.35	English	11.25–11.35	break
9.35–9.50	break	11.35–12.20	French
9.50–10.35	history	12.20–13.10	physical education (PE)

Mimi starts school at 8.05 a.m.

So liefen die Übungen:

3

Über einen Tagesablauf berichten

Ein Bericht ist eine sachliche Wiedergabe eines Geschehens. Folgende Punkte sind wichtig, um einen guten Bericht zu verfassen:

- Gehe in deiner Beschreibung Schritt für Schritt vor. Was ist zuerst passiert, was kam danach? Überlege auch, ob der Ort oder bestimmte Personen für deine Beschreibung wichtig sind.
- Achte darauf, dass du bei allen deinen Sätzen die gleiche Zeit verwendest. Wenn du im Nachhinein über etwas berichtest, verwendest du das *Simple Past*.
  Beispiel: First, I had breakfast.
- Damit sich dein Bericht flüssig liest, verwende unterschiedliche Satzanfänge.
  Beispiele: afterwards, then, after that, first

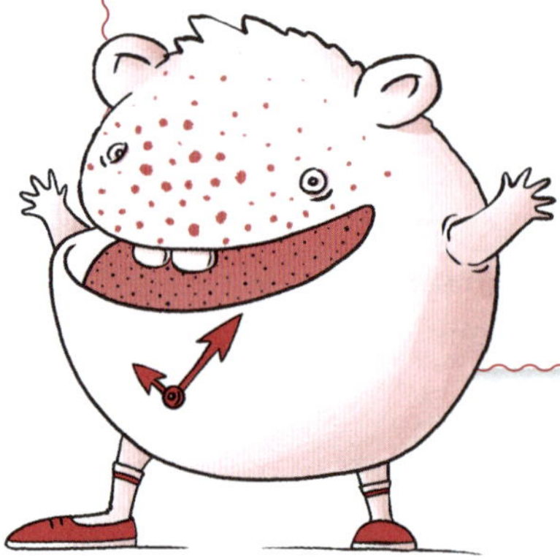

1 **Hier ist etwas durcheinandergeraten. Schreibe die Sätze richtig.**

breakfast / have / I

____

teeth / my / I / brush

____

I / to school / the bus / take

____

my / do / homework / I

____

lunch / have / I / at noon

at seven o'clock / get up / I

go / I / to the playgroundd / at 3.30 p. m.

dinner / I / have

2 **Nimm nun die Sätze aus Aufgabe 1. Bringe sie in die richtige Reihenfolge und setze die Verben in die richtige Zeit. Verwende auch Wörter wie *afterwards, then, after that,* damit dein Text flüssiger wird.**

So liefen die Übungen:

3

Eine Unterhaltung schreiben

Wenn sich zwei Personen abwechselnd miteinander unterhalten, nennt man das einen Dialog *(dialogue)*. Solche Gespräche sind im Alltag ganz typisch, zum Beispiel beim Einkaufen oder in der Familie. Auch in einem Gespräch kann man über etwas berichten. Wovon handelte der Film oder wie war das Ende des Buches? Ein Dialog beginnt häufig mit einer Begrüßung, am Ende steht eine Grußformel.

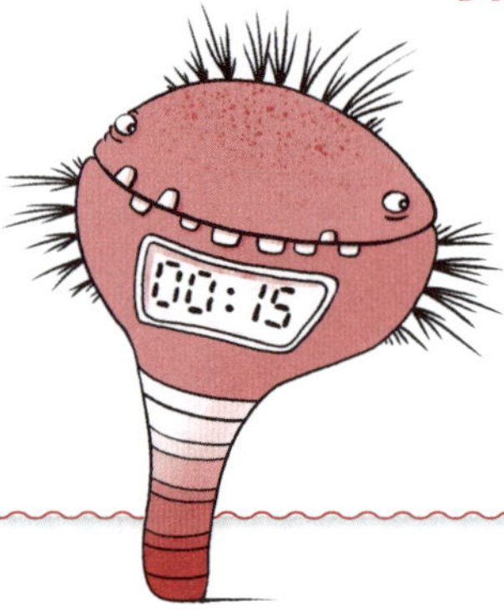

Beispiele: "Good morning, Mrs Smith."
"Good morning, Sarah."
"How are you?"
"I'm fine, thanks. How are you?"
"Great. Thanks."

"Hello Mary. Come in, please."
"Thank you. Nice to meet you."
"Nice to meet you, too."

1 **Übersetze!**

Hello! ______________________________

Have a nice day! ______________________________

Hi there! ______________________________

Welcome! ______________________________

Good bye! / Bye-bye! ______________________________

2 **Hannah kauft auf dem Markt ein. Schreibe die richtige Grußformel in die Lücke. Tipp:** Schau bei Aufgabe 1 nach.

Hannah: "______________________, Mrs Rose."

Mrs Rose: "______________________, my dear."

1 2 3 4 5 6

Hannah: "Could I have two kilos of potatoes, please? And that's all for today."

Mrs Rose: "Of course. Here are the potatoes. That is 2.10 €, please."

Hannah: "There you are. Thank you very much. ______________________."

Mrs Rose: "______________________ . ______________________."

3 **Schreibe zwei Dialoge. Verwende einige der angegebenen Begriffe.**

a) **book – what is it about – it's mine – interesting crime story – should read it – thank's a lot – you're welcome**

Mary: "Look! There's a book on the floor. Whose ______________________

____

Sarah: ____

____

Mary: ____

b) **why – watch – TV show – together – favourite actor – interesting guests**

Mum: "Why do you watch this TV show?"

Tim: ____

____

Mum: ____

____

So liefen die Übungen:

_ _ _ _ _ _ _ _ _ _ _ _

Vom Urlaub erzählen

Es gibt sie immer noch: Postkarten – kurze Grüße vom Urlaubsort, freundliche Botschaften zur Aufmunterung. Postkarten haben auf der rechten Hälfte Adresszeilen, da schreibst du den Empfänger hin.

Auf der linken Seite ist Platz für deinen Text. Den Text beginnst du immer mit einer persönlichen Anrede. Nach der Anrede schreibst du im Englischen immer groß weiter.
Beispiel: Dear Mum/Grandma/Paula,

Danach kann du von deinen Erlebnissen berichten. Schreibe zum Beispiel, was du den ganzen Tag lang machst, wie das Wetter ist, welche Pläne du hast oder wann du zurückkommst.
Beispiel: On Monday, I will visit the local theatre.
The weather is amazing.

1 **Sarah schreibt eine Postkarte aus den Sommerferien. Fülle die Lücken aus. Aufgepasst: Manche Lücke muss auch leer bleiben!**

afternoon – breakfast – fantastic – towns – ice cream –
Dear – fine – Love – play – have – go

____________ Jason,

How are you? I'm ____________ . Italy is great. The weather is ____________ . In the morning, we usually ____________ a big ____________ . After ____________ breakfast, we walk to the beach and ____________ for a swim in the ocean. In the ____________ we sometimes go to little ____________ by bus. We ____________ sit down in one of the cafés and have some ____________ . In the evening we often

____________ cards. Sometimes we play table tennis.

____________ , Sarah

2 **Schreibe nun deine eigene Postkarte!**

So liefen die Übungen:

____

4 Erklären

Ein Rezept schreiben

Koch- und Backrezepte erklären einen Vorgang ganz genau, ähnlich wie eine Gebrauchsanweisung. Wichtig dabei ist, dass man die Reihenfolge einhält und keinen Arbeitsschritt auslässt.

In Rezepten wird genau erklärt, was man tun muss. Sie sind im *Imperativ* geschrieben.

Beispiele: *Mix the flour, the sugar and the salt.*
Melt the butter.
Stir in the milk.
Spread (ausbreiten, verteilen) *the dough.*
Sprinkle cheese on top of the pizza.

1 **Hast du schon mal eine Pizza belegt? Überlege, in welcher Reihenfolgen die Arbeitsschritte erfolgen müssen, und schreibe die richtigen Zahlen in die Kästchen.**

- ☐ Prepare the pizza dough.
- ☐ Spread the dough on the baking tray.
- ☐ Cover a baking tray with baking parchment.
- ☐ Enjoy!
- ☐ Cover your pizza with tomato sauce, mushrooms, peperoni, garlic, olives or whatever you like.
- ☐ Sprinkle mozzarella or grated cheese on top of the pizza.
- ☐ Preheat the oven.
- ☐ Bake the pizza in the oven. Be careful not to burn it.

2 **Schreibe die Sätze aus Aufgabe 1 nun in der richtigen Reihenfolge auf. Achte darauf, dass du keinen Schritt auslässt.**

____

____

____

____

3 **Wer isst was am liebsten? Schreibe auf, was die verschiedenen Personen am liebsten auf der Pizza essen, und zeichne es auf.**
Tipp: Du kannst auch verrückte Zutaten, zum Beispiel Schokolade, verwenden.

My friend likes ______

My mum loves ______

______ only eats ______

I like ______

So liefen die Übungen:

______ ☺ 😐 ☹

4

Eine Gebrauchsanweisung schreiben

Bei einer Gebrauchs- oder Handlungsanweisung schreibst du einen Vorgang für jemanden in einzelnen Schritten auf. Mithilfe der Anweisungen soll ein Dritter ohne weitere Hilfe zum Beispiel richtig Zähne putzen oder ein Spiel spielen können.

Verwende in deinem Text möglichst aussagekräftige Verben, die den Vorgang plakativer erscheinen lassen und dem Leser genau sagen, was zu tun ist.

Beispiele: *open* – öffnen, *close* – schließen, *put away* – wegstecken, *rinse* – ausspülen, *brush* – bürsten, *need* – brauchen, *shuffle* – mischen, *put down* – hinlegen, *reveal* – aufdecken, *turn around* – umdrehen

1 **Marie erklärt ihrer kleinen Schwester, wie sie richtig Zähne putzen soll. Wie lautet die richtige Reihenfolge? Nummeriere die Kästchen.**

- ☐ Now smile and remember to go to the dentist twice a year.
- ☐ Healthy teeth make a nice smile.
- ☐ Brush your bottom teeth first.
- ☐ Brush the biting surface, too.
- ☐ You need a toothbrush and some toothpaste.
- ☐ Put some toothpaste on the brush.
- ☐ Brush in small circles, first the outside of your teeth, then the inside.
- ☐ Then brush your top teeth in the same order: outside, inside, biting surface.
- ☐ Brush your teeth two times a day.
- ☐ It is therefore very important to brush your teeth.

2 Beschreibe die Regeln des Memospiels, bei dem man immer zwei gleiche Motive finden muss, für einen Freund. Verwende die Wortbausteine.

put cards on table – turn them around – shuffle – show same picture – back side up – look for two matching cards – reveal cards – take the pair – your turn again – the other player's turn – if the pictures don't match – most pairs at the end – win

Take the cards and shuffle them.

____

____

____

____

____

____

____

____

____

____

____

So liefen die Übungen:

______________ ☺ 😐 ☹

5 Argumentieren

Pro und Kontra

Dafür oder dagegen? Beim Argumentieren geht es darum, eine Meinung zu begründen – also klar zu formulieren, warum man für oder gegen etwas ist.

Für eine Argumentation brauchst du **gute Gründe** für oder gegen eine Sache. Manchmal musst du zu einem Thema auch beide Seiten betrachten. Überlege dir wichtige Gründe und notiere diese. Präpositionen helfen dir dabei, deine Gründe noch besser zu formulieren.

Beispiele: *first of all* – vor allem, *besides* – außerdem, *in addition/additionally* – zusätzlich, *because of* – aufgrund, *in spite of* – trotz/trotzdem, *nevertheless* – dennoch

1 **Überlege dir Argumente für und gegen ein Geschwisterkind.**

It is good to have a brother or a sister because …

____

____

____

____

I like to be a single child because …

____

____

____

____

2 **Gehst du gerne in den Zirkus? Überlege, was dir daran gefällt. Fülle die Mindmap aus und nutze die Wörter in deinem Text. Argumentiere für oder gegen den Zirkus.**

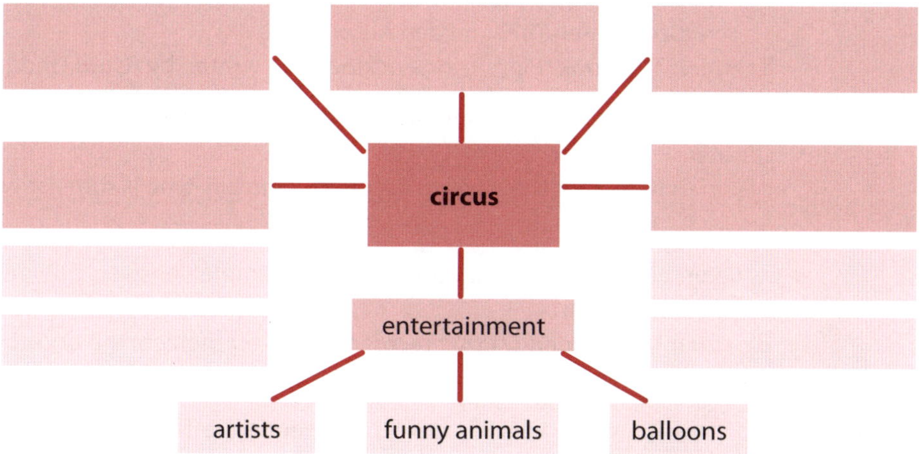

So liefen die Übungen:

5

Eine Buchbeschreibung erstellen

Buchrezensionen beschreiben ein Buch, seine Handlung und die Vor- oder Nachteile. Man findet sie in Zeitungen, Zeitschriften und im Internet. Wer eine **Buchrezension schreiben will,** …

- … nennt zuerst den Titel und den Autor.
  Beispiel: The book "Pippi Longstocking" was written by Astrid Lindgren.
- … fasst das Geschehen zusammen, ohne den Ausgang der Geschichte zu verraten.
  Beispiel: It is about the adventures of a young girl, who is super strong and who …
- … liefert eine Begründung, warum das Buch empfehlenswert oder nicht empfehlenswert ist.
  Beispiel: I recommend / don't recommend (= empfehlen) the book because …

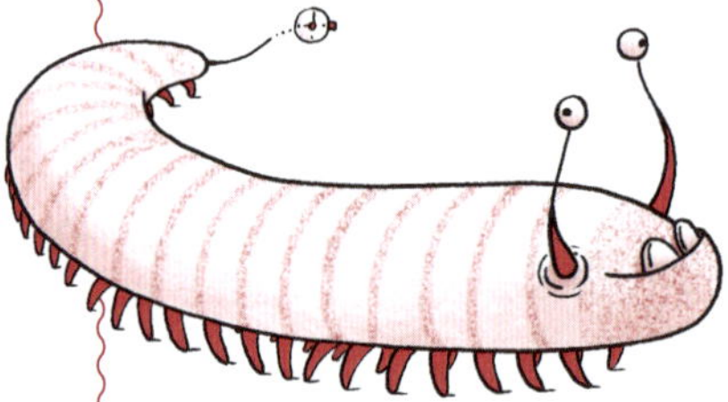

- … verwendet treffende Adjektive.
  Beispiel: interesting, funny, too long, boring, exciting

1 **Welche Adjektive passen zu den einzelnen Bucharten? Nutze die Wörter aus dem Wortspeicher und überlege dir andere Adjektive, die ebenfalls passen.**

romantic – fascinating – interesting – old fashioned – exciting – boring – funny – thrilling – magic

A love story can be ______________________

A fairy tale can be ______________________

Fantasy novels can be ______________________

A detective novel can be ______________________

Historical novels can be ______________________

2 **Schreibe ein *Book Review* zu deinem Lieblingsbuch.**

Title and Author: ______________________________

____

What's the book about?

____

____

____

____

____

My favourite character …

____

____

____

____

____

I like the book because … / I cannot recommend the book because …

____

____

____

____

So liefen die Übungen:

____

6 Erzählen

Eine Geschichte schreiben

Geschichten bestehen in der Regel aus vier Bausteinen:

1. der **Hauptperson** beziehungsweise den **Hauptpersonen.** Auf Englisch nennt man sie *character(s).*
2. dem **Ort** des Geschehens, man nennt ihn im Englischen *setting.*
3. einem **Problem** oder einem **besonderen Ereignis,** welches die Hauptpersonen erleben.
4. der **Auflösung** *(solution).* Schließlich braucht das Problem eine **Lösung** beziehungsweise das Erlebnis ein Ende. Die Auflösung bildet den Abschluss der Geschichte.

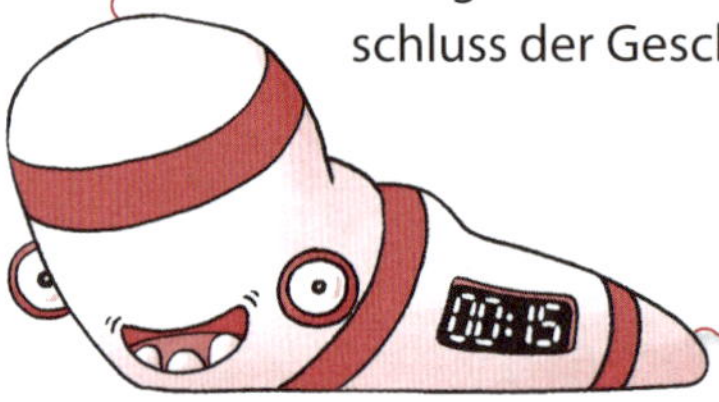

1 **Aus diesen vier Puzzlesteinen setzen sich die meisten Geschichten zusammen. Schreibe die folgenden Begriffe auf das passende Puzzleteil:**

at school – Mia – after the break, the purse is in Mia's school bag – misses her purse – can't buy snack

1 2 3 4 5 6

2 **Lies und schreibe die Geschichte weiter.**

Today is Monday and Mia is at school. The math lesson is over and Mia is looking forward to the break. She wants to buy a chocolate bar at the kiosk. She opens her school bag, but she can't find her purse. "But I remember that I took it to school this morning." Mia is unhappy, but her friend Sarah helps her out. Sarah buys two chocolate bars.
Tara watches Mia and Sarah. This morning she found a purse in the girls' restroom. What if the purse is Mia's?

She ____________________

So liefen die Übungen:

____

6

Wissenswertes über Märchen

Märchen *(fairy tales)* sind schon immer beliebte Geschichten. Sie zeichnen sich dadurch aus, dass darin wunderliche, magische Dinge geschehen. Die meisten Märchen fangen an mit den Worten **Es war einmal – *Once upon a time …*.** Auch kommen **magische Zahlen** wie die 3 oder die 7 vor. **Beispiele:** *The seven ravens* (Die sieben Raben), *Snow White and the Seven Dwarfs* (Schneewittchen und die sieben Zwerge)

In Märchen gibt es auch oft Tiere, die sprechen können *(Frog King),* und natürlich **Zaubersprüche** *(abracadabra)* oder **magische Gegenstände.** Achte darauf, diese besonderen Märchen-Elemente zu verwenden, wenn du ein Märchen nacherzählst, veränderst oder neu schreibst.

1 **Verbinde das Wort mit der passenden Erklärung.**

fairy tale	Zauberer
dragon	Zauberstab
spell	Hexe
wand	zauberhaft, magisch
magic (adj)	Fee
magic (noun)	Drache
fairy	Zauberspruch
witch	Zauberei, Magie
sorcerer	Märchen

2 **Kennst du dich mit Märchen aus? Kreise die richtigen Antworten ein.**

a) Cinderella loses … a necklace / a shoe / a ring.

b) In the fairy tale "The wolf and the seven little goats" the wolf eats one goat / six goats / seven goats.

c) Sleeping Beauty wakes up after ten years / one hundred years / one thousand years.

d) The Queen gives Snow White a sandwich / some chocolate / an apple to eat.

e) Bremen's Town Musicians are a goat, a dog, a cock, a cat / a donkey, a dog, a cock, a cat / a goat, a dog, a cat, a fish.

f) The Frog King marries his frog mate / a princess / a dragonfly.

3 **Überlege: Wodurch zeichnen sich Märchen aus? Schreibe vollständige Sätze in das Fairy Tale Fact Sheet. Die angegebenen Wörter helfen dir dabei. Ergänze auch noch eigene Ideen.**

king – queen – castle – dragon – prince – princess – witch – forest – cave – a magic wand – fairy – elf – sorcerer – once upon a time

Fairy Tale Fact Sheet

Beginning sentence: ______________________________

____

Magic characters: ______________________________

____

Magic creatures: ______________________________

____

Magic places: ______________________________

____

Magic things: ______________________________

____

So liefen die Übungen:

____

6

Ein eigenes Märchen schreiben

Es war einmal … Märchen schreibst du am besten in der Vergangenheit, im Englischen im *Simple Past*.
Regelmäßige Verben bilden das *Simple Past*, indem man ***-ed* an die Grundform** anhängt.
Beispiele: look – looked, walk – walked, talk – talked

Unregelmäßige Verben musst du auswendig lernen.
Beispiele: eat – ate, ride – rode, shine – shone

1 **Schreibe ein eigenes Märchen. Verwende Begriffe aus der Tabelle, um den Lückentext zu füllen. Nutze deine Fantasie!**

Magic charac-ter(s)	A magic place	Magic animal or object	A reason to act	A surprise person	The solution
king queen prince princess witch sorcerer elf fairy	a castle a tree-hou-se a ruin a hidden cave an aban-doned villa	a golden key	love envy happiness / unhappi-ness curiosity a promise a curse a reward	gardener another prince / princess a child …	marriage death a big party …

Once upon a time there was / were ______________________________

(magic character(s)).

He / She / They lived in ______________________________ (magic place).

One day, the ________ lost __________________________ (magic object).

______ was extremely unhappy and promised a big reward for the person who would bring back ______________________ (magic object).

The next day, a foreign prince knocked at the entrance door of __________

______________________________________ (magic place).

He ____

The __________ was happy again. As a reward, __________ gave the prince

______________ . And they lived happily ever after.

2 **Erzähle ein bekanntes Märchen neu, indem du es veränderst. Wähle dafür eine der beiden Ideen aus. Wenn dir der Platz nicht reicht, nutze ein separates Blatt oder ein Heft.**

a) Cinderella loses her smartphone / the prince can't find her / time passes / they meet again years later

b) Snow White meets the seven dwarfs / they give her super powers / evil stepmother tries to poison Snow White / she …

____

____

____

____

____

____

____

____

____

So liefen die Übungen:

______________ ☺ 😐 ☹

Lernkalender

Kapitel	Seite	Zeit	☺ 😐 ☹
Wörter sammeln	4		
Auf den Satzbau achten	6		
Richtige Zeiten verwenden	8		
Ideen und Gedanken ordnen	10		
Täglich schreiben	12		
Spielerisch mit Sprache umgehen	14		
Eigene Texte korrigieren	16		
Eine Person beschreiben	18		
Einen Gegenstand beschreiben	20		
Gegenstände und Personen vergleichen	22		
Die Lage von etwas beschreiben	24		
Einen Ort beschreiben	26		
Ein Hobby beschreiben	28		
Einen Weg beschreiben	38		
Einen Steckbrief erstellen	40		
Uhrzeit und Datumsangaben	42		
Über einen Tagesablauf berichten	44		
Eine Unterhaltung schreiben	46		
Vom Urlaub erzählen	48		
Ein Rezept schreiben	50		
Eine Gebrauchsanweisung schreiben	52		
Pro und Kontra	54		
Eine Buchbeschreibung erstellen	56		
Eine Geschichte schreiben	58		
Wissenswertes über Märchen	60		
Ein eigenes Märchen schreiben	62		